## Praise for
## *When She Leaves Me*

"*When She Leaves Me* is a field of wildflowers that blooms after raging fires scorch the forest. These poems not only refuse to let sorrow and destruction have the final word, they are in fact only possible because they are born from that charred past life. In this collection, Gorman shows us how when we damn near break our necks for years trying to salvage a life, it's only in letting go that we're truly saved."

-Armin Tolentino
  author of *We Meant to Bring It Home Alive*

"*When She Leaves Me* conjures a 'story of so much breaking,' weaving together the shattered pieces of a marriage to illustrate how we build myths about our relationships, the ones we love, and even ourselves. The writing is stripped bare and raw, a gut punch that reflects the devastation felt when one is left to find their way and 'rebuild with old planks, failed projects, unfulfilled plans.' The vulnerable honesty of this collection reveals not only the unspoken realities hidden behind social-media-ready posts, but also the deep-down and, sometimes, buried strength we find to move on."

-Lydia K. Valentine
  author of *Brief Black Candles*

"Raw, tender, honest, and real, Benjamin Gorman's *When She Leaves Me* slips in like a blade between 'the bones of joy / and mourning' and cuts straight to the heart. Gorman invites us to listen to 'the story / of the choice / to tell / this story,' the story of the end of a marriage, and of his determination 'to see it / the way / it is,' even as what he comes to see more clearly is himself. Within these pages, Gorman lights a fire beneath 'that thing / you are not allowed / to say,' refining and transmuting this pain to hope. Read this to feel more human. Read it to live a little louder. Read this for the courage to become your own alchemist."

-Bethany Lee
  author of *The Breath Between: An Invitation to Mystery and Joy*

"*When She Leave Me* is a visceral tour through the shards of life and love. This is a passionate reminder that all the facets of our lives are important, fragile, worthwhile and, unfortunately, impermanent. Benjamin Gorman captains us through a tossing sea full of rainy love, tempestuous truths, monstrous introspection, and gray-scale rainbows. This doesn't have a hero; it's not supposed to. But it's alive, very, very alive, and because of that, it roots and attaches around your heart."

-Zack Dye
  author of *21$^{st}$ Century Coastal American Verses*

"This collection is a shoot-from-the-hip storytelling of the complexity of love, marriage, parenthood and divorce. Gorman's voice bravely explores the pain that comes with the realization that ending what was meant to be a lifelong relationship at times is the best happily-ever-after one can hope for. I honestly couldn't put this work down. I totally loved it, and you will too."

-William V.S. Tubman III
  author of *Anthem Mantra Light: Poetry/Inspiration*

# When She Leaves Me

a story told in poems

by Benjamin Gorman

**Novels by Benjamin Gorman**

*The Sum of Our Gods*

*Corporate High School*

*The Digital Storm:
A Science Fiction Reimagining of
William Shakespeare's The Tempest*

*Don't Read This Book*

# When She Leaves Me

a story told in poems

Copyright © 2020 by Benjamin Gorman

All rights reserved.

Published in the United States by
**Not a Pipe Publishing**
www.NotAPipePublishing.com

Hardcover Edition

**ISBN-13: 978-1-948120-70-8**

## Dedication?

For Cupid
you capricious little prick

*"Poetry
brings
present
that
which
is
apart"*
-Bethany Lee

*"Every writer must articulate from the specific. They must reach down where they stand, because there is nothing else from which to draw."*
-Gloria Naylor

*"I have found that contempt, derision, and misdirections for those asking questions of the powerful are often symptoms of deep fears for the truth that could be exposed."*
-Dan Rather

*"We read to know we are not alone."*
-C.S. Lewis

# Contents

| | |
|---|---|
| Teaser | 1 |
| Prologue | 2 |
| Shipwrecked | 4 |
| When She Leaves Me | 6 |
| Cannot Try | 7 |
| Spark | 8 |
| Poetry | 9 |
| Christmas Lights | 10 |
| Polyhedron | 11 |
| Shrink | 13 |
| Cold | 14 |
| Bad Geometry | 15 |
| Therapeutic | 16 |
| She Says | 17 |
| Done Hiding | 18 |
| Blame | 19 |
| Drowning Wrong | 20 |
| Shell | 21 |
| Whittling | 22 |
| Lawn Leftovers | 23 |
| Simple | 24 |
| Broken | 25 |
| Strange | 26 |
| Bed | 27 |
| Lucky | 28 |
| Taste | 29 |
| Shoulder | 30 |
| Status Update | 31 |
| Kindness | 32 |
| Dig | 33 |
| New Theory | 35 |
| Now | 37 |
| Tense | 38 |
| Lacking | 39 |
| Weighting Priorities | 40 |
| Unsupported Column | 41 |
| I Meant It | 42 |

| | |
|---|---|
| Comforting | 43 |
| Used To | 44 |
| Unconscious | 45 |
| True | 47 |
| Hair | 48 |
| Translation | 49 |
| Facial | 50 |
| Bio | 51 |
| Again | 51 |
| Obligation | 52 |
| Hope | 54 |
| Dislocated | 55 |
| Ambition | 56 |
| Crazy-making | 58 |
| Irrational | 59 |
| Growing | 60 |
| Bent | 61 |
| Bad Day | 62 |
| Unsaid | 63 |
| Seriously | 64 |
| Ashes | 65 |
| Don't Stop | 67 |
| Soundtrack | 68 |
| Happier Birthday | 69 |
| Preparation | 71 |
| Swipe | 74 |
| Maybe Friends | 75 |
| She Says He'll Be Fine | 77 |
| Pictures | 79 |
| Interested | 80 |
| Online Dating Profile | 81 |
| Visitation | 83 |
| Warnings | 85 |
| Wending | 86 |
| Completely Authentic | 88 |
| Truth | 90 |
| Dancing Alone | 91 |
| So What | 92 |
| Voyage | 93 |
| Defeated Reading | 94 |

| | |
|---|---|
| Schrodinger's | 95 |
| Cuyahoga | 98 |
| Signs and Slams | 99 |
| Gravity | 101 |
| Dreaming | 102 |
| Forgiveness Is Telling Myself a New Story | 103 |
| Friends | 106 |
| Daydream | 107 |
| Sometimes a Pepper Grinder | 108 |
| To the Audience Across the Lawn | 110 |
| About the Author | 113 |

## Teaser

(5/11/19)

This is the story
of the choice
to tell
this story

## Prologue

I am no Prospero
freeing Ariel from one bondage
and locking him in another
or Faust
calling up Mephistopheles
and entering into negotiations.
Your Chorus is more like Odin
making the first people
from an ash and an elm
and naming them
Ash and Elm.
Not very creative
this time.
I have drowned my magic books.
I have only honesty.

Our characters,
the couple I conjure
were married for 19 years
happily, I thought
when she announced
she didn't want to be married to me anymore.

She made this confession
in Costa Rica
    Costa
    Fucking
    Rica
when I was trapped in a hotel room
4,359 miles from comfort.
so I made the mistake
              of sharing it with the world.

Back home
after we started meeting
            with the divorce attorney
I begged.
She decided to stay.

I un-announced.

But I worried.
So I started writing poems
in secret
about my fears
hoping they would never be read
because she'd stay.

Spoiler.
You're reading this.

# Shipwrecked

(11/29/18)

Once, in the land of Ecrovid,
                      a man found himself
              chewing on fish bones
      he'd plucked from a pile of ashes on the beach.
He stared out into the blue
    under blue
        under blue
and thought of his son across the sea
                          in need of a father,
            of all his supportive friends,
and the inappropriate,
      sometimes amusing support from strangers,
          like the two laughing boys riding a camel
who invited him into the desert to forget
or the woman who showed him a picture of herself
                kissing a different stranger
            and didn't explain why
or the turtle who had surfaced
while he clung to the broken mast.

The turtle had said he would be fine
    if he could only get to the beach beyond the sunset
        because that's where baby turtles come from.
It made no sense to the man
      but nothing did.
So when the three mountains
    peaked over the horizon
          he'd followed the turtle's directions.
    But the beach was empty.
And all the strangers

       shouted kindnesses from a great distance
about the beauty of certain parts
                of the land of Ecrovid
          places he could not reach.
    And no one rescued him.

He thought about the storm while he chewed the bones.
She had come upon the boat so quickly
      Striking with lightning.
    Sinking with efficiency.
You cannot be angry at storms
           for being storms.
        Or at ashes for tasting
              like ashes.
           Or at innocent fish
               consumed by
                   long dead fire.

## When She Leaves Me

(12/16/18)

When she leaves me
she will never enjoy
the sad songs
in her collection
in the same way
because she'll hear
an echo

## Cannot Try

(12/16/18)

She can't be expected to try
to feel
what she could not help
but unfeel

## Spark

(12/16/18)

They call it a spark
because it should
start an engine.
But sparks vanish
faster than

## Poetry

(12/16/18)

She never liked
poetry
especially free verse
even when
she announced
she needed something outside
our rhythm.

She will not
like
this.

## Christmas Lights

(12/16/18)

You test the string
before you put it up.
All the little fires
promise
to fight
against the darkness.
You make the precarious climb
to make a house
warmer.

Then, one day
a single strip is cold and dead.

You do what you can.
You tinker and replace.
You change.

But the power will not flow
The sparks there are gone
Nothing to be done.

You're powerless
also.

Loving her
is
that.

## Polyhedron

(1/23/19)

Pushed into
this new shape
with many sides.

She says it's not
something I lack
just something more
they can offer.

A need she must satisfy
but not a failure of mine.

Only addition.
No subtraction.

A shape
with many faces
but honest.
An ethical polyhedron.

I honestly
do not understand
this kind of mathematics.

If I cannot bend myself
into this shape
isn't that a lacking?

If I'm looking at the shape
the wrong way
isn't that a failure?

I suspect
she'll reject
this square.

# Shrink

(1/23/19)

The problem
           I'm told
is my anxiety.
Why won't I trust
that she won't leave?
Just because
she was going to leave?
Now she says she won't.
The professional
turns the dial.
The aperture constricts
to focus on my fear.
The cause
is out of the frame.

## Cold

(2/27/19)

I
am
awake.
She is so
close but she
wants to sleep so
I'm stuck lying here
but I'm not allowed to
converse about this with
anyone because it's just too
private so I craft my nightmare
while painfully aware that it's very
lonely in the bed we still are sharing.
And cold.

## Bad Geometry

(2/27/19)

Shape not taught in
geometry:
Her solution,
polyamorous,
does not equal
polyamorous,
if it's one sided.
Then monogamous
doesn't equal
amorous.

# Therapeutic

(3/14/19)

"And unfortunately, we are out of time,"
he says
at the end of all our sessions
and I can't help but think
it's too
on
the
nose

## She Says

(4/2/19)

She says
she doesn't want me to see it that way
and I thought
she meant
it isn't that way
but
she doesn't want me to see it
because she doesn't want to see it
the way
it is

## Done Hiding

(4/10/19)

When I was young
and wanted to be
as masculine as I thought I was supposed to be
I used to hide from sadness
by choosing anger.
Rage was easier to express.

Now sadness comes easily.
Maybe too easily?
And when I run out
that's where the anger hides.

## Blame

(4/11/19)

Now she realizes
why she wants to leave me.
The new reason:
I didn't do the dishes enough
I ruined a vacation 14 years ago
One evening I wouldn't stop playing video games with a friend.

I own these. I am to blame.
These things built up over time
she says
and she never let them go
and now she resents me
too much.

But I can't tell anyone this new story
because it would make her look bad.

It should make her look bad.
She is more worried about looking like a villain
in the eyes of others
than she is
about breaking me.

But I must remain silent to save us.
so if you're reading this

## Drowning Wrong

(4/13/19)

I thought we were two drowning people
who agreed to help each other
stay afloat.
I was wrong.
It turns out
I was trying to cling to a log
who was really a resentful shark.

## Shell

(4/18/19)

I can't tell
      if I'm healing
from the outside in
      or trying not to explode
from the inside out.

# Whittling

(5/2/19)

For 20 years
learning
point the blade away from myself

Then 20 years
    20 fucking years
carving out her happiness

And she didn't like the piece
    of art.

So now I have to be selfish
to make myself into something new
not my choice of a subject
    No choice.
But it's hard to break the conditioning
and turn the blade on myself.

## Lawn Leftovers

(5/5/19)

    Sometimes
you get tired of having a lawn
or the lawn gets tired of you.

Don't focus on how that rejection feels.

Accept it: The lawn is tired.

So you rebuild
with old planks
    Failed projects, unfulfilled plans
and a layer of peat
    Lawn leftovers
and then black plastic trash bags
    Detritus and mourning
and then topsoil
    Mostly shit
and then holes
    Aching and open and vulnerable
and you plant a garden.

It's too early to say
    It's beautiful.

But
if it grows
    If
it will be better.
    Maybe.

## Simple

(5/6/19)

She says I'm making it too simple
expecting an explanation.
It's complicated.

No.
It's binary.
A one or a zero.
Leave or stay.
She made that choice.
She made it simple.

Working it out
would be complicated.
Leaving without explaining why?
Simple.

# Broken

(5/9/19)

I thought she broke me forever
and she did but
not in the way I thought.

She broke us apart
and there was a way I held her
a kind of embrace
an encompassing respect
a cocoon of veneration
which has not survived.

And this was part of me
as much as my own arms around her
so I am cracked because
she has broken free from me
and she is broken to me.

I will heal.
She may already be healed.
She will never be to me
what she was.

# Strange

(5/10/19)

It's strange
how quickly
she becomes a stranger.
And it's stranger
to realize
she may have been growing strange
for years.

I know
my need to be known
has always been strange.

I feel this strange pull
in this strange time
to be a stranger to everyone.
But why, if she is a stranger
must I become a stranger
when her strangeness
burns so?

I know now
that I will fight
to be known.

**Bed**

(5/11/19)

My queen-sized bed is

                    far
        too
empty.

I wonder when I'll
   be able
   to touch

                    her
side.

## Lucky

(5/13/19)

For two decades
I joked
I was the lucky one.
That she settled for me.

She didn't
reciprocate.
Not so funny anymore.

But now I see
she was lucky, too.

She has decided
she does not value
what I have to offer.
I am not worthy of her.
but when someone
won't tiptoe through her eggshell forest
honor her graveyard silences
stumble through her fog of uncertainties
and he breaks her heart
she may remember
I would never have done that.
That's something
she gave up.

**Taste**

(5/13/19)

So I am no longer to her taste.
So be it.
I do not want to hurt
the woman I have loved for 22 years.
But she no longer wants to be that person.
This new person?

    It's only ink on paper.
    just ink on paper
    ink on paper but

she will not like the flavor

## Shoulder

(5/13/19)

My son's shoulder
is strong
enough to hold up
his father's head.
But he should not
have to carry this.
I worry about him.
She dismisses this.
Says he'll be fine.
I find this
incomprehensible.
It's not just his family.
She broke his father.
How does she think
that will go?

## Status Update

(5/14/19)

She's leaving her husband of 20 years.
So, to celebrate
she's gone off to Cabo
for a girls' week
over Mother's Day.

As one does.

I shit you not.

**Kindness**

(5/17/19)

I continue
to show her kindness
in a thousand little ways
she will not recognize
in memory
of the time
before she was so cruel.

I do not know
why.

## Dig

(5/17/19)

Dig
can be a noun
when referring to the place
where the digging is done.

I have become a dig.

I must go deeper
and figure out
what is left of me
under the rubble.

First it's mostly manure
so many lies
plopped unconsciously
but still steaming.

And then
stone
the foundations of systems
of pressing down
to level.
So many ninety degree angles
I didn't push against.

And then more stone but
made of the corpses
the shells
the homes
of ancestors so small
their failed marriages are
mercifully forgotten.

And then a heat
and pressure
of molten iron
that could be
all this anger but also
love just waiting
to break
the surface.

## New Theory

[5/18/19]

I don't yet know
the reason.
She won't tell me.
But I just had a thought.
A hypothesis
maybe.

Imagine if a person
Spent hours
and hours
and hours
and hours
and hours every week
   primping
   straightening
   tweezing
   applying
   lifting weights
   making shakes
   and documenting it all
so she could look good
to others
because she already
looked beautiful to her husband
without all that effort.

No matter how much he appreciated
the result of all that work
she knew he would love her without
any of it.

At some point

she might start to resent
love that wasn't dependent
   on a flat stomach
   and silicone bags of self esteem
   and skin that didn't show
     signs of motherhood
   and hair just
     so

Maybe she needed
someone else
who needed her
to look like
someone else.

# Now

(5/19/19)

She gave me the reasons.

I was off fighting the good fight
   and she wanted me to come home to her
      but she didn't want to say so
         because she believed in the work.

And then it was too late.

Odysseus comes home
   and Penelope welcomes him back
      but why shouldn't she hate him?

She doesn't hate me
   but it's too late to change
      the past.

         The past has sunk us.
        Our history is Charybdis.
     We sailed too close.
  No demigod could pull the tiller hard enough
To escape now.

**Tense**

(5/19/19)

I could scream
Why didn't you care enough to tell me?
She could scream
Why didn't you care enough to guess?
In our house
we never raised our voices
so it's all
past tense.

I still care enough to try now.
I can scream.
She doesn't.
So she can't.
The end.

## Lacking

(5/19/19)

among the many things I lack:
the maturity to hear long discussion
on the quality
of fish tacos

Also:
the grace to wear a smile
and hear her tell us
about the cool guys
met on a getaway to Cabo
over Mother's Day
two weeks after she told him
she was leaving his father

## Weighting Priorities

(5/19/19)

I didn't notice
she was carrying that suitcase.
That's my fault.
She decided not to drop it.
That's hers.

I kept tossing my resentments onto the side of the road
Apple cores
Banana peels
The pits of plums
I thought they were biodegradable.

Now I feel tempted
to go back and find mine
so I can have
as heavy a bag
out of spite.

No.

I can choose to keep walking
without mine.
She decided she would have to
carry hers forever.

Now that she's on her own road
will she be calloused by that weight?

## Unsupported Column

(5/19/19)

The next time
she's in a relationship
and she feels unsupported
and lonely
and resentful
maybe she will say:
"I feel unsupported"
"I feel lonely"
"I feel resentful"
They will be happier.

But why should she take
relationship advice
from me?

And why would I give it?

# I Meant It

(5/20/19)

I used to say
I love you
every night
and I meant it.

Now I say
I'm sorry
and mean it.

All the pain I caused
is not excused
by my ignorance.
I failed.

And
(not but)
and

She didn't love me back
not really
and she can't apologize for that
not really.

## Comforting

(5/20/19)

I guess
when I tried to reassure her
by saying
"I'll never leave you"
I thought that was a promise
she'd find comforting
but to her
it started to sound
like a curse

## Used To

(5/20/19)

After she announced
she was leaving me
the first time
then changed her mind
I used to
fear I'd come home
to an empty house.

I would have wailed.

She regretted shocking me
so she's drawn it out
for months
and months.

As she lingers
and I see
every day
what she doesn't see.
About us.
About her.

Maybe that's her strategy
to soften the blow.
If so
my respect for her
now wanes.

## Unconscious

(5/21/19)

I thought
it was just
her personality.
I knew
she was not
affectionate.
I didn't know why.
I didn't know.

She didn't either.
She was unaware
that she felt distant
that she resented me
maybe from the beginning.

She didn't know
she was making me feel alone
because she felt alone.

She didn't mean
to exact
revenge
for her isolation.

She didn't intend
to deceive me
when she said she loved me
back then
or when she said she'd try to rebuild
after.

She doesn't know

that she is hurting our son
by giving up on his father.

She is ignorant
of my loss of respect.

The quantity of her obliviousness
fills a universe
of empty space
between us.

# True

(5/22/19)

This morning
she expressed
a small frustration
then said
"Sorry
"I shouldn't have said anything."

No.
She should have been sharing these
for the last twenty-two years.

I said,
"How's that for irony?
Not wanting to say anything
is what got us here
and now we don't want to say anything
because it won't make a difference
when we could actually be more honest
than ever
because it won't make a difference."

She only replied:
"True."

# Hair

(5/23/19)

When she leaves me
my first project
will be a deep cleaning
of my house.
My house.
I would like to remove
all her hair.
This seems funny to me now.
It will not be funny
when I find a strand
in two years
and sob.

## Translation

(5/23/19)

There is a subtext
to all our current silences.
I am whispering,
"It's not too late
to turn back
from this terrible thing you're doing."
And she is saying, flatly,
"I know."

## Facial

(5/23/19)

I wonder
how long it will take
for the shopping algorithms
to stop blasting me
with the kinds of items
I used to buy for her.
The artificial intelligence
is dumb
and hurtful.

## Bio

[11/30/18]

Sometimes you have to update all your bios
because you don't get to have
that particular life
anymore

## Again

[5/24/19]

Sometimes you have to update your bios
again
because you thought you'd get to have
that particular life
again
and then you don't anymore
again

# Hope

(5/24/19)

I suspect
my son will reflect
that his childhood
was happy
and loving
and quiet.

My co-parent and I
gave him that.

He is now
at the age
where I start to hope
I've parented
in a way
that will give a better
childhood to my
grandchildren.

I document
a transcript
of the silences

He can review when he's ready.
I want my son to keep
all the happiness
all the love
but maybe make
my grandchildren's childhoods
louder.

## Dislocated

(5/25/19)

I've arrived
at forgetfulness
a place where just enough
has been accepted
to allow moments of happiness
followed by remembering.

In between
there's a confusion
a dislocated joint
that would still work fine if only
the bones of joy
and mourning
could be shoved one into another
with some cartilage of sense.

# Ambition

(5/26/19)

I've always been
The ambitious one.

> "We have to admit,"
> they whisper
> "It seemed strange
> "that she was so cold to you."

I have a new hope.
What if?

> "You need to be careful,"
> he warns
> "because when you find somebody
> "who loves you
> "you aren't going to be used to it."

Imagining
a different her.
Someone who sees me
and smiles
and wants to reach out
and take my hand
who kisses me when she can
and wishes she could kiss me when she can't

> He's right.
> Even if someone were
> totally wrong for me
> To be loved
> To be loved
> To be loved
>       Wholly.
> But what if she's right for me?

        Holy shit.
To think
To think
It's even possible.

## Crazy-making

(5/26/19)

It's not quite gaslighting
if it's unintentional
but there is a
degree of obliviousness
that's dangerous to
others' sanity.

# Irrational

(5/26/19)

A more rational person
would calculate
that her opinion
of his physical appearance
is no longer
relevant.

I wonder
how long it will take
before I am insensitive
to her disregard
for my insecurities?

no longer hypersensitive to
her casual
derision?

# Growing

(5/26/19)

While she packs boxes
the trees we planted in the backyard
keep growing.
I will stay and guard them.
We will bear fruit.

## Bent

(5/27/19)

After a windstorm
one of the largest blooms
in my rose garden
hangs his head
despondent.
He'd grown too large
comfortable and ambitious
and fragile
I was certain
he'd lose his petals
and die.
He will, eventually.
But he's surviving
in that humbled pose.

# Bad Day

(5/27/19)

Note to self:

Any future significant other
must be the kind of person
who generally responds to a stressful day
by reaching out to me
as a source of comfort
rather than pushing me away
like I'm an additional irritant
or tiresome to-do.

This is a deal-breaker.

## Unsaid

(5/27/19)

That thing
   you are not allowed
     to say?
             Hold it tight.
Squeeze until you
   plant it into the flesh of your palm.
Let its vines wrap around your pen
     and grow a poem.

# Seriously

(5/28/19)

    She sat down
    and complained
        to me
about the annoying difficulties she endured
                buying furniture
      for the new apartment
    she'll move into
when she leaves me.

    Seriously.

Either she's too oblivious
        to consider
   how this cuts me
or she knows.

# Ashes

(5/30/19)

Never having had cause
to mourn like this before
    (Such a charmed life
    so happily married
    unprepared)
I'd heard people talk
about how
after losing loved ones
food tastes like ash.
Hyperbole, I thought.

In the months after Costa Rica
(Costa Fucking Rica)
I lost 30 pounds.

There wasn't much to me before
I have always been
insubstantial
slight
lacking presence.

I became a wraith.
Then I was fooled into
eating again.

Deceived into happiness
is still happiness.
The calories don't
judge her veracity.

Now I am diminishing again.
Shrink while

chewing
ashes.

# Don't Stop

(5/30/19)

Don't stop.
Write through it.
Isn't there a meeting I should attend?
An essay to grade?
Find another tiny weed sprouting in the garden.
Smoke another cigarette.
Anything. Anything.
Don't stop and feel this.
The gentle stream becomes a fetid pool
home to a blanket of algae
and the squirming larvae of mosquitoes
if it loses momentum.
I can't know when
my marriage started
to stop
stopped moving
started smelling
rotting
dying
but I won't follow suit.

## Soundtrack

(5/30/19)

I should not have come to this.

I'm not ready.
I'm here for him
    listening to middle schoolers
    sing sad songs about
    feelings they don't understand
While I sit next to
    the woman who taught me
    a new kind of pain
    more off-key
    sharp
    and flatter
    than any spine-jarring note
    through an anxious, quavering,
    strained windpipe.

This is the soundtrack
    to our co-parenting
    a film about
    a radioactive armrest.

## Happier Birthday

(6/1/19)

How do I say
                Happy Birthday
when I don't think she should be
quite as happy
as she seems
and I'm not glad
it's her birthday?

                                      Behind me
two decades of
                Happy Birthdays
stolen by her implication
that she wasn't ever truly happy
that my efforts to bring her joy were failures.
How can I know?
How can I ever know?
I spiral
   needlessly
      pointlessly

And maybe this can be a turn
out of the whirlpool
It doesn't matter anymore
if she was unhappy but didn't say so
or happy but changed her mind
to escape
She has snatched her happiness from me
She doesn't get to care if I care

So maybe I can let go
leave the foggy history
in the letters in the file cabinet.

And start to write
about who I want to become
without the compromises
and who I want to find
and what real love might feel like
on a
                      Happier Birthday
in a different season

# Preparation

[6/2/19]

A failure of imagination led
To thinking of myself as unprepared
Unearned, my blessings raised my unbowed head
And Death, so busy elsewhere, fam'ly spared
To face my own naivete, so clear
My innocence revealed as weakness still
When privilege is counted up, I fear
Averted gaze rather than swallowed pill
What kind of loss could ascend to this height?
My parents, siblings, child are live and hale
And comparing divorce to death seems slight
For surely one does make the other pale
Now I recall some other tears and sighs
Another set of scales fell from my eyes


My crib was built in Christendom's vast land
The church, the pleasant garden where I grew
The coffee hour with every shaken hand
The sermon and the potluck both as true
Unquestioned this devotion carried on
Through hymns all sung unheard and prayers banal
From Babel, Jericho, to Babylon
Misunderstanding, noise to break the wall,
Then exile from my mind, the Temple Mount
Diaspora, my skepticism passed
When zealotry inflated my account
Of faith, so many mustard seeds amassed
So certain was I of this old god's grace
Became I merely Sin before His face.

And still this wretched creature could not stay
And love this old white Dad with beard and hair
Americans want heaven just their way
The streets of gold have blinded people there
So Doubt became my new god for a time
I worshiped Her with all my soulless heart
But She can't teach a poet how to rhyme
Destruction is Her one and only art
The faithless do not gather to share song
Or break our bread in vast and storied halls
Our love a clashing cymbal, clanging gong
No holy days to order springs and falls
I did not lightly cast away belief
It was, till now, my source of greatest grief


Oh, Irony, so bitter and so sweet
In grief I picked up paper and my pen
And served my time upon the writer's seat
To craft a novel, one long joke, and then
Of all the people in the world, my wife
Encouraged me to publish that first book
And make my old strange hobby my new life
The parallels demand a closer look.
Just as my loss of faith, a time device
Went back, my precious soul to steal away
By showing it was never there, lost twice
So she has proved willing to inveigh
Against her love for me so that it, too,
In doubt is lost to memory's dim view



To that great height, idolatry, I let
Her vaulted in my estimation rise
Till like some ancient temple's minarets
She was more fair more distant from my eyes
And like that tower she withheld her gifts

Affection she was soon loathe to bestow
And who can blame a goddess for such thrift?
No blessings grant for those so far below.
A touch, a kiss, a smile became as rare
As miracles of the old testament
But all my failures catalogued with care
My supplications she grew to resent
To this disparity I remained blind
It's only in her leaving that I find


That feigned indifference is just as cruel
As genuine disdain, both share a root
The gears can grind you down on either fuel
A love that's fake is just like one that's mute
I'm more prepared than I did understand
I lost my way before and found one new
There is no god my fate can now command
No goddess who can tell me what is true
The god and goddess treated me the same
Withheld, demanded yet to be revered
I've learned to own my anger without shame
I'll find my peace when both have disappeared
I've felt more loss for god who may not be
Than she has shown as she's discarded me

## Swipe

(6/4/19)

                        She will be
                                                      different
                        She will not
hide from politics
                        She'll create
                                                              art
not melodrama
                        She'll want to
                                    sit across a candle flame
                                      and talk about books
                        She won't
reject the gift of a poem
                        She'll curl up
                                            in a blanket
                                          with me and a movie
                        She won't curate
a museum of my failings

                        More than anything
                                           she'll fall hard
not hard pass

                        I have to be careful
                        Make sure she's not
                                          different
just to be different

# Maybe Friends

(6/8/19)

I remember a show I watched.
There was a
   character
a really likable guy
and he was in this
Will They / Won't They
until the writers dodged
a series ending happy conclusion
by revealing
after
   twenty-one
      episodes
that he'd been a spy all along
and a villain.

She told me
after
   twenty-one
      years
she suspected
   maybe
she's never really loved me
but
   maybe
she'd stayed with me because
she wanted to be my friend.

I don't think she's a villain
but
   maybe
someone who would do that
to someone she wanted to keep as a friend

    maybe
doesn't have the
    character
I thought she had
and
    maybe
isn't a friend I should keep.

## She Says He'll Be Fine

[6/9/19]

She attempted to relieve
my concerns about our son's chillier
cavalier attitude that underlies
his steelier withdrawal
when she plied me with
her antalkalies for my alkaline worries.

At first I believed
her replies
about his resilience,
the homilies she supplied
I thought were salient,
stories of earlier families
who have rallied
when sullied by similar
marital alienation.

And he has not confronted us with contumelies,
but remained the princeliest complier
while my normally brawlie mood
grows uglier.

But now I believe the likeliest situation
is that his ebullient demeanor
is like flies who overlie
the oiliest spot in some lilied pond
waiting for a timelier moment
to explode into panoplies of gallied flight
to take grizzlier action to fill their bellies
on the blood of some fleshlier passerby
before buzzing off to earthlier environs.
He has every right to be snarlier

and this right multiplies daily.

I consider the milieu in which he lives
All the lies she has told
Lies to me
Lies to him
Because she lies to herself.

    And I think it's a good idea
    for one of us to worry about him
    honestly.

## Pictures

(6/9/19)

Tonight
I thought it wise
to take pictures
of all the pictures
of the three of us
when I thought we were
a happy family
in case she takes those pictures
with her when she goes
to her next happy family.

# Interested

(6/9/19)

I thought
this was the story
of the choice
to tell the story
of her leaving.

But that's not it at all.

This isn't for her.
She is
    disinterested.

When she leaves me
she will not hear sad songs
and think of me.

This is a story
for someone who may
read the poems and want to know me.
This is the story for the woman
who will cup my face in her hands
and look into my eyes
and say, "I read the poems
and already understand you
better than she does
because I want to know you.
I am
    interested."

This is my story to tell
and I'll tell it
for someone
who cares.

## Online Dating Profile

[6/10/19]

The whale shark
is not a whale
and that isn't his fault.

He was
misnamed.
I didn't choose to be dating either.

He feeds by
opening the huge mouth
at the end of his 62 feet of
simple skin
and inhaling.

Most online dating profiles are written
with the same urge to
open up as wide as possible
to capture the whole school.

I only want to find
one person
who will hike with me through the woods
and march with me for people who aren't as lucky
and sit across a table and laugh with me
and, when she stops laughing,
suddenly smile at me with a flash in her eyes
as eager and grateful and hungry
for my company
as I am for hers.

A whale shark
who only wants to find

one fish in the sea
is very empty.

# Visitation

[6/12/19]

Radio signals
pass through space
and time.
Some start
at the beginning
of the universe
and will continue
to the end.
Others are
interrupted.
We will see
each other
again.
And then
less
and
less.
Troughs and spikes
of a longer
waveform
will
thin
until I am no longer
angry
at not knowing
she stopped seeing me
a long time
ago.
Maybe
all the way back
to the beginning.
So maybe

a few degrees
of rage
will radiate
forever.

# Warnings

(6/12/19)

They've already started to shout
over the sound of the waves
water crashing on pebbles
so many tinkling keyboards
telling me not to share
not to publish
keep this to myself
be silent.

They are loving and kind and good and well-intentioned
They do not understand me.

They do not know why
        we place these
            words together
              one after another,
                  fitting just
                      so.
                  A writer
              attempts to
            build a bridge
    from an island prison.

They do not mean to tell me to stay there.
They cannot hear themselves over the waves.

They do not realize
They are not telling me what I should not do.
They are telling me that I should not be.

## Wending

(6/14/19)

This path is thin and uneven.
I have to choose each footfall
Carefully
Carefully
    Turn
Let my son love his mother
    Twist
Avoid telling her how I'm feeling about her now
    Bend
Not complain about her to my friends too much
and drive them away
    Curve
Not pretend that everything is fine too much
and drive them away
    Hairpin
Not fall over the side
    into the steep cliff
      where this anger is a thousand jagged rocks
     that puncture as I bounce and try to
     hold their bloody points
      because letting all the rage go means
       falling further and faster
      into an abyss
Not overcorrect
    and stumble
    into a river of false forgiveness
    its surface so placid and inviting
    its bed blanketed in the hooks of dead trees

　　　　its strong current of virtue and guilt
　　　　pushing all genuine feeling
　　　　　　　　　　　　down
　　　　　　　　　　　　down
　　　　　　　　　　　　down
This path is thin and uneven.

## Completely Authentic

(6/14/19)

Today she says,
"I know I'm moving out
but that doesn't mean I've stopped caring completely."

   "Completely."

We agree.
It's not the moving that means that.

She employed me as her builder.
to build her relationships with others
to fabricate the love she couldn't show between us.
For twenty-two years
I did that work for her because I believed
there was love under there
love that could be housed.
Love she felt but couldn't show.

Then she fired me.

At our exit interview
she told me she
         maybe
never loved me.

Caring people do not
dig holes under the foundations of the houses they have
asked others to build
smash the load bearing columns

set the frame on fire
even if it's just to ignite an excuse
to run out of a burning building.

She said she has to end us
destroy another relationship
leave
to be her authentic self.

I believe her.

## Truth

(6/15/19)

A single statement  
Can be simultaneously true  
And difficult to believe  
Like when a friend tells me  
"You're better off without her."

## Dancing Alone

(6/16/19)

Went to a concert with some friends
and saw a beautiful woman
dancing alone
throughout the entire show.
I almost worked up the courage to talk to her.

(At the end
it turned out she was with
the band's drummer
of course
it's always the drummer.)

But still
when I was
dancing alone
I almost worked up the courage to talk to her.

Still alone.
But dancing.

## So What

(6/17/19)

So what
if she can't fully apologize
and I can't fully forgive?
We can hold one another
and say goodbye
and become strangers
instead of enemies.
I am on the downhill side now.
stumbling towards
healing.

## Voyage

(6/27/19)

The trip
from

"Please
please stay.
I'll do anything
Just, please."

to
(never within earshot)

"Get out.
Pack up all your shit.
Take all the pictures of yourself.
Getoutgetoutgetoutgetout!"

is a long and exhausting journey.

But I have arrived.

## Defeated Reading

(6/29/19)

Reading a novel
about soldiers
who stop believing
they can win
so they stop soldiering
and lose
and I can't help but think
of a mental health counselor
who refused to get her own counseling
or do the work in couples counseling
or get a counselor afterwards.

It's not my business anymore.
But she haunts my reading.
I thought I was further
in my own story.
I'll discuss it
with my new counselor.

# Schrodinger's

[7/1/19]

I've spent a lot of time today
   contemplating
Schrodinger's cat.

This hypothetical cat
  is in a box.
There's poison in the box.
The poison will be released
 when a detector senses
  the decay of an atom
   but until we open the box
    we don't know if the cat is
     alive or dead
        so
   it's alive *and* dead
  until we open the box
 and the two states
become one reality.

She will not ask me
   why I am still angry.
     That's the box.
So I can't tell her something
   that might really help her,
     an antidote to the poison.
I want to tell her
 her love is
  Schrodinger's cat.
   She may care about other people.

She may have loved me.
But she kept that inside.
She loved *and* didn't love.
Maybe she is kind and good and caring.
Maybe not.
If it's in the box,
it's a quantum superposition
of love *and* not love.

If, for 19 or 18 or 17 or 10 or 5 years
she had loved openly
and then the love had died
it would have hurt
but we both would have known
love, *then* not love.

Writing on the outside of the box
"This is half your fault."
"You should have known."
Insult *and* injury.
Killing/not killing a cat
and
trying to share the blame.
She's forgotten all the times
she said she would try to love me
and tried/not tried
a quantum superposition of effort.

The injury is why I'm getting over her,
moving on faster than I thought I would,
finding kindness
and maybe even love
can exist
outside the box.

Some people
    I'm learning
        can care about me
           openly.

The insult is why I'm still angry.

## Cuyahoga

(7/3/19)

A paper airplane
when made incorrectly
can sail through a light, airy loop
and crash, nose first
without starting a fire.

The Cuyahoga River
burned at least 13 times.
It was made so wrong
it just kept burning.
Even small disappointments
set me smoldering
convinced I will never
flow correctly.

Tomorrow I will get on an airplane
and fly off to stand
on the banks of the Cuyahoga.
It's repaired now.
There is life under its surface.
Perhaps it can convince me
I will not burn forever.

## Signs and Slams

(7/4/19)

"You don't really know someone
until you don't know someone"
my cousin Sally tells me.
And you don't know
you chose not to see it
until you see it.
Curves can be subtle
turning points unnoticed.
There were signs.
When she got
a little too into
her new mantra
"No fucks to give"
way past the point of humor
a religious devotion
to apathy.
And when she learned about
the INFJ doorslam
and got so excited.
Sure, it's fun to learn something about yourself
but description is not prescription.
She missed the signpost
saying "Warning
Bad Habit
Abrupt shoulder
Dangerous cliff"
instead embracing a fault
as an identity.
That was a sign

I missed.
My fault.
She's on the other side of the door now.
She can slam her doors
and slam and slam and slam
until she's in her comfortable closet
enjoying the perfect bliss
of not giving a fuck
about anyone.
My anger rebounds.
Why was I so blind
to the screaming signs?
Keeping my head down
my hope for our happiness
as much a delusion
as her concern for me.
I cannot hate her
but I can hate
that little part of me
that still loves her.

## Gravity

(7/6/19)

Gravity
is not constant.
Some days
certain facts
weigh more than they should.
    It will never be fair.
    I will never understand.
    I will never
    stop wishing
    we could be friends.
But gravity will change tomorrow.
These facts will be lighter.
Others will take on mass.
Someday
someone else will matter more
and happiness
will be a neutron star.

That does not change
the weight
today.

## Dreaming

(7/25/19)

For most of my life
I could awaken
from a nightmare
and take comfort
in her presence.

Now I awaken
confused
and rediscover
her absence.

Waking is not a nightmare
anymore.
I open my eyes and sit up
to enter a life that has become
a foggy dream
where nothing makes sense and
I heal by growing comfortable with that
where the plot does loops
a surreal, meandering quest
sometimes stuck and sometimes moving
searching or waiting to be found
by someone better who
thanks to inexplicable dream logic
will care enough to stay.

## Forgiveness Is Telling Myself a New Story

(8/6/19)

This manic joy
washes over me.
Eureka.
Epiphany.
Relief.

I spent decades
plugging this narrative
into vacuum.
Generously
I presumed she had
a rich inner life.
It made all her silence
"I love you"
but all her thoughtlessness
at the end
willful.

My storytelling
caused
my pain.

But I have a new
generous
possibly false
story I can tell myself.

What if there wasn't much
going on in her head

at all?
The acts of thoughtlessness
were just that.
The lack of caring
just a lack.

She's not stupid.
I thought she avoided conflict
with others
out of social anxiety
but maybe her impulse
to keep everything simple
and routine
is just discomfort
with inner conflict.

This is my new story of her:
When the going gets tough
she prefers not to think about it.

So she wasn't being willfully thoughtless
just thoughtless
and I can stop blaming her
for what she couldn't do.

I thought I couldn't forgive her
for the hurt she caused
but I can forgive this new her.
And I can forgive myself
for being too
generous
to her
by being too
generous

to her
and myself
and learning to love
my stupid optimism.

Better:
I worried I couldn't tell this story
and I'm liberated
by the new her.

Don't worry about these poems hurting her.

She won't read this far.

And I've already found
better friends
who will.

# Friends

(8/13/19)

"Is it alright
if we're still friends with her?"
my friend asks.
"Please,"
I say,
"She will need friends,"
I say,
"I won't be responsible
For taking you away."

I don't say,
"But don't expect much in return
unless you are a novelist
who is inclined to create the story
that she cares about you.
And even that
will only work
for so long."

## Daydream

(8/15/19)

I fell asleep on my couch
and dreamed
she brought my son home
and saw me sleeping there
and woke me up, just to say hi

and I sprang up and started shouting
"Get out! Get out, get out, get out!"
But before she could even flee
I said,
"Oh. So sorry. I was only half-awake
and thought I was reacting
to a recurring dream."

and she accepted my apology
but gained some insight
into how much she hurt me
and where she stands
in my nightmares.

None of this would ever happen
but it was a pleasant dream.

## Sometimes a Pepper Grinder

(8/24/19)

I discovered
  she left the salt grinder
    but took the pepper grinder.
  I joked there might be metaphor there.
This offended her.
"Sometimes a cigar
is just a cigar," she said,
"and sometimes a pepper grinder
is just a pepper grinder."
I looked away
  and bit down hard on a smile
    because she couldn't see
     she was saying the pepper grinder
    meant nothing to her
   and something to me
 so now she'd made the metaphor
perfect.
     More perfect
      because she couldn't see it.

Months ago
    I thought I would never find this all funny
     until I was happily sinking
      into the arms of someone new
       who rakes her nails across my skin
      because she wants to hold on to me
    so badly.
  I was right about that, too.

This metaphor

is now
 fucking hilarious.

## To the Audience Across the Lawn

(7/1/19)

You see it.
A pillowcase with dried salt stains.
A t-shirt with darkened armpits
from that family hike.
A sweatshirt with snot on it.
Is that at the height of her nose where
I held her while she cried?
Or on the sleeve where I wiped my nose
and disgusted her?
Both.
And it gets worse.
Pants with dirt on the knees and
Is that manure on the thighs?
Yes. We planted many gardens.
And those sheets!
That's clearly vaginal fluid and semen.
Yep. That, too.
And baby puke and baby food and those little baby cereal
puffs that melt to goo under and between everything?
Disgusting!
Believe it or not, that was the best part.
You see it and wonder
why would he hang such
dirty laundry out to dry?
For you.
This is for you.
This is a life. The messes and stains
aren't the sermon,
just the scripture.

The lesson is:
Hiding it
kills it.
So let your stains sing.
Make your messes shout.
When you love
grab that hand
even when yours is clammy.
Or dirty
or dusty
or defiled.
It won't be cleaned
through contact.
It won't be baptized.
It will be sanctified.

## About the Author

Benjamin Gorman is a high school English teacher. He lives in Independence, Oregon, with his son. His novels are *The Sum of Our Gods*, *Corporate High School*, *The Digital Storm: A Science Fiction Reimagining of William Shakespeare's The Tempest* and *Don't Read This Book*. He believes in human beings and the healing power of their stories.

# Also Available from Not a Pipe Publishing

## Brief Black Candles
### by
### Lydia K. Valentine

"In *Brief Black Candles*, Lydia Valentine attends, with passionate velocity, to questions of survivability, remembrance and the creative art of living a fully human life, even in contexts and conditions that work against that what-it-could-be. ...reading becomes a mode of witness. ... Haptic, revolutionary and unflinching, this is a powerful debut collection by a poet who does not, and cannot, 'in this time-/ in this place-', look away."
  -Bhanu Kapil

"This debut collection, written in the most truthful key available to language, uses poetic form and precise repetition to give shape, then echo, to questions of family, loss, justice and survival, seated in the frame of an America that is a long way from post-racial—the America of today."
  -Sanam Sheriff

**Wherever Fine Books Are Sold**

## Also Available from Not a Pipe Publishing

# Strongly Worded Women

The Best of the Year of Publishing Women
An Anthology
Edited by
Sydney Culpepper

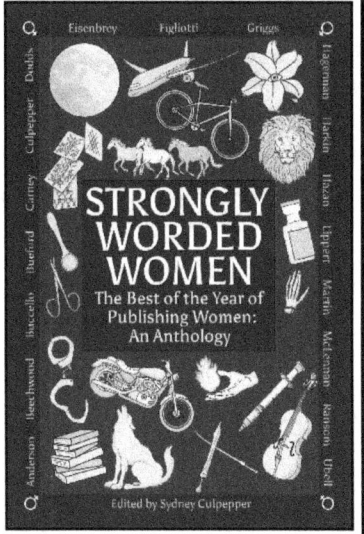

With stories by Maren Bradley Anderson, Debby Dodds, Jean Harkin, Laura Hazan, Lori Ubell, Chloe Hagerman, Lizzy Carney, Tonya Lippert, Claudine Griggs, Taylor Buccello, Julia Figliotti, Rosie Bueford, Elizabeth Beechwood, LeeAnn Elwood McLennan, Heather S. Ransom, Sydney Culpepper, and Karen Eisenbrey

Back in 2015, Not a Pipe Publishing announced accepting author Kamila Shamsie's challenge to the publishing industry to only publish women authors in 2018. After publishing eight novels by seven authors, they capped off their Year of Publishing Women with an anthology of 18 short stories by these amazing women authors from across the country.

**Wherever Fine Books Are Sold**

# Also Available from Not a Pipe Publishing

## Shout

### An Anthology of Resistance Poetry and Short Fiction

Edited by Benjamin Gorman and Zack Dye

With poems and short stories by **Rosanne Parry**, **Janet Burroway**, **Carolyn Adams**, **Benjamin Gorman**, **Lydia K. Valentine**, **Zack Dye**, **Rebecca Smolen**, **Eric Witchey**, **Heather S. Ransom**, **Joanna Michal Hoyt**, **Stephen Scott Whitaker**, **Karen Eisenbrey**, **Meagan Johanson**, **TJ Berg**, **Jennifer Lee Rossman**, **Carlton Herzog**, **Austin Case**, **Allan T. Price**, **K.A. Miltimore**, **Jill Hohnstein**, **Kurt Newton**, **Taliyah St. James**, **John Miller**, **Christopher Mark Rose**, and **Bethany Lee**.

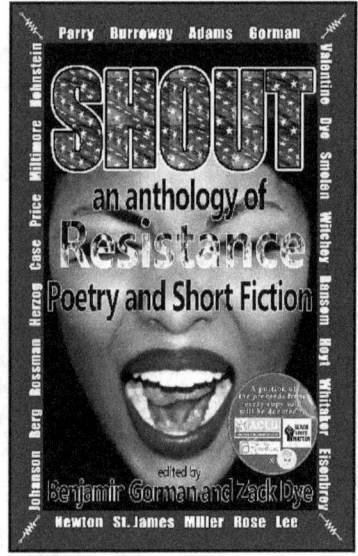

The 25 incredibly talented authors and poets in this anthology aren't politicians, policy wonks, or partisans. They're artists staring at the rising tide of fascism in the United States and asking you:
"What kind of world do you want to live in tomorrow?"
and "Who do you want to be today?"
And they aren't asking quietly.

**Wherever Fine Books Are Sold**

# Also Available from Not a Pipe Publishing

## Djinn
### by
### Sang Kromah

Bijou Fitzroy is strange.

As an empath, she has spent her entire life as a recluse, homeschooled by her overprotective grandmother, never allowed to stay in one place long enough to settle down and make friends. When Bijou and her grandmother move to Sykesville and she starts to attend the local high school, Bijou's world begins to crumble, town locals begin to disappear, creatures from her nightmares come to life, and she finds herself at the center of a secret war fought all around her.

"Sang Kromah weaves a tale rich in drama and TV melodrama! This is *Buffy* on acid, with all the colorful characters one would expect and more. Twists and turns - and twin heartthrobs - had me hooked from the start. A saga for the ages, and the teenagers."
  - Micayla Lally
    author of *A Work Of Art*

**Wherever Fine Books Are Sold**

**ALSO AVAILABLE FROM NOT A PIPE PUBLISHING**

# Don't Read This Book
### by
## Benjamin Gorman

Magdalena Wallace is the greatest writer in the world. She just doesn't know it.

When she wakes up chained to a desk next to a stack of typed pages and the corpse of the person who read them, she learns just how dangerous her book can be. Rescued by a vampire, a werewolf, and a golem, she's on the run with the manuscript — and the fate of humanity — in her backpack, and a whole lot of monsters hot on her heels!

"…a whimsical, fast-paced, delight; snappily written, deliciously funny and smart, and full of affection for its characters."
- New York Times bestseller Chelsea Cain, author of *Heartsick*, *Mockingbird*, and *Gone*

"... smart, determined, and filled with really stunning prose ... maybe one of the best books I've read!"
-Sydney Culpepper
 author of *Pagetown*, editor of *Strongly Worded Women*

**Wherever Fine Books Are Sold**